Praise for Joshua Peralta's

3RD & ORANGE

"*3rd & Orange* is finely bruised nostalgia that is excellent for the soul. Peralta's words will make the world fade away for an afternoon. It is a touching, truthful book."
—Steven T. Bramble, *Disposable Thought*

"Joshua Peralta's collection *3rd & Orange* perfectly captures the effervescent eye of a young man exquisitely attuned to each cloud and to every shared cup of coffee in his California cityscape. His work embodies those charmed moments in a lifetime when we find ourselves so easily able to say: Yes, I belong here, this matters."
—Susan Hansell, Founding Editor of *SpotLit*

"*3rd & Orange* is a portrait of a time and place, caught in arresting detail. It's also a portrait of a time and place in the author's life, a moment that many of us have experienced—poised between the before and after of the onset of adulthood, between potential and realization. My heart ached and sang simultaneously reliving these years."
—Mike Guardabascio, Co-founder of *The562.org*

3 R D *&* O R A N G E

J O S H U A   P E R A L T A

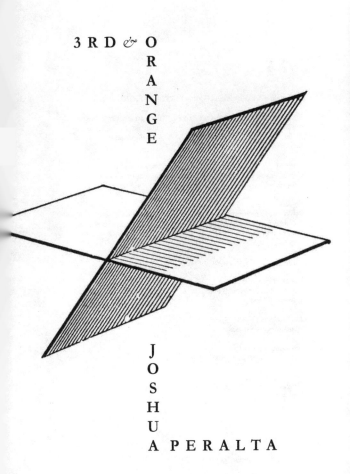

ZQ-287

LONG BEACH   OAKLAND

3rd & Orange

Published by
ZQ-287 PRESS
Long Beach, CA

Copyright © 2022 by Joshua Peralta. FIRST EDITION.

Except for a few lyrics from Otis Redding's "Cigarettes & Coffee" (written by J. Butler, E. Thomas, and J. Walker) and the short quotations at chapter breaks, all text herein is the original work and property of the author.

Some of this collection originally appeared elsewhere in different versions. Sincere gratitude to the editors of the following journals and websites who saw in my work something fit to print:

Rip Rap
("Balloon as Reminder" & "Sunken City", originally titled "Listen" 2005; "Sound of Swallowing", originally titled "Sometimes the Sound of Swallowing" 2006)

Ariel
("It Begins Like This" 2006)

Spot Literary Magazine
("On Unhurried Evenings Like This" & "Returning at Dusk from a Walk in the Hills" 2007)

The Good Men Project
("Underdog" & "Ambition" 2014)

Spry Literary Journal
("The First Days" June 2015)

Bird's Thumb
("Bioluminescence" 2015, nominated for a Pushcart Prize)

Saga Literary Journal
("Dinner Guest" and "Oracle of the Open Heart", Spring 2021)

joshuaperalta.net

Cover and Interior Design: Steven T. Bramble

ISBN: 978-1-7325766-3-6

All rights reserved. No part of this book may be reproduced or transmitted in any form or by any means, electronic or mechanical, including photocopying, recording, or by any information storage and retrieval system, without the written permission of the Author or Publisher, except where permitted by law. For information address: ZQ-287 Press/ Steven T. Bramble, Long Beach, California.

for
you

Preface

A broken heart is a hard thing to come back from. We tend to crawl off and stay down for a while, feel bad, and attempt to have others pity us while we lick our wounds. We may even partake in a few short, meaningless physical encounters or superficial friendships. We drink a lot.

In the time I have known the author of this collection, which amounts to a short lifetime getting longer, I have watched him make such a comeback.

I have been a neighbor to Josh, an enemy, a thorn in his side, a coworker, and a friend. Mostly the latter. I suppose this gives me an insight to these poems deeper than most, as my own evolution (or devolution) has taken place alongside their development. I am even a focal figure in a few of them.

I cannot help but to think that the places we reside play a crucial role in our mending or further unraveling each time we come undone. Needless to say, the people with whom we share our lives are even more essential to these processes. The following poems attest to that notion.

I have had the privilege of receiving some of these in their infant stages, sometimes in emails or letters or on napkins in a bar. This would never have happened had Josh and I not lived in the same town, Long Beach, California, at some time or another. I am now excited to see that they have not been quietly filed away, but published for public view.

In these poems I see the various apartments Josh lived in, the couple of serious relationships he had, the meals we made and ate together, and the bitterness of each beer we drank while inhabiting Long Beach. The darkness of various bars on 4th Street illuminates some back region of my mind, and evenings we spent in either of our apartments discussing books, music, bullshit or Bangkok are not just re-lived but actually animate this work. I imagine anyone who reads these poems will get the sense that they are all at once a personal lament and celebration of the distances the author has traveled both within and without himself.

I am sure he will publish other things, perhaps further collections of his stories and poems. Whether they will amount to few or many I cannot say. What I am positive of is that the quality of their content will surpass this collection. However, they will not be as significant. The writing in this slim volume returns me to a time and place I will, regretfully and to my chagrin, never get back. At the same time, they remind me that going forward without dismay about the past is an immovable mountain. What else are we left to do but climb?

I congratulate my friend on the publication of these very special poems. And I am envious of you, reader, who gets to read them for the very first time.

—Mark Canett, 2020

contents

backward.................................9-14

3rd & Orange.........................15-30

Orange & 3rd.........................31-54

3rd & Junipero......................55-66

Elm & 3rd.............................67-90

Atlantic & 3rd......................91-102

forward...............................103-114

afterward............................115-166

backward

~

And I shall drive my chariot down your streets and cry
Hey, it's me, I'm dynamite, and I don't know why
And you shall take me strongly in your arms again
And I will not remember that I ever felt the pain

Van Morrison
"Astral Weeks"

The First Days

We moved in together the day after the first day of summer. We carried box after box up our stairs and stacked them against the bare walls of our new old apartment. We made the place ours, filling empty closets with clothes, filling blank shelves with books and knickknacks, mingling yours with mine.

I remember the slow process of unpacking. One-by-one, delicately as an archaeologist delivering mysteries from the earth, you lifted items from your boxes and reflected. I remember you unwrapping a replica of Degas' *Little Dancer*, which your father gave you before he left. Your fingers loosened her newspaper bandages while you told how she came by her chipped chin. Box by box for a week like this, we shared the intimate histories of our things. Summer rolled on, and our new life came together as easily as if we had dreamed it.

I remember the incredible ease of Sunday mornings we didn't work. I remember the crisp symmetry of waffles forked from my mother's old iron griddle, battered yet dutiful after decades of breakfast. I remember the texture of Talavera mugs, dimpled and full of fresh dark coffee.

I remember fireworks blooming over the harbor in sparkling cyan, lemon white, kiss red. Their explosions lit the sky around us, flashing over the streets and alleys and illuminating the beach below the cliffs. From our balcony, we watched with mouths agape, gasping like kids with each bright burst.

I remember coming home from work early one evening on a Saturday in late July. I tip-toed up the stairs to sneak up on you. Instead I found you sprawled in the middle of the living room, asleep in the warm drowsing light. Curled beside you, your cat picked her head up and yawned, slunk over to me, and the two of us left you napping. Later you woke to the pop of a cork and a purpling sky. You called my name like a question mark and wandered toward the sound. You found me with the cat in my lap on the balcony reading a book of stories, waiting with two cups of red wine and a headful of fine ideas about what to do with our delicious night.

I remember the smothering heat of August and the utter incompetence of our ceiling fan. I remember throwing open every window in our apartment, heaping curses on the heads of our landlords, on the crazy hearts of lunatic neighbors, on the mosquitoes that buzzed in our ears and fattened themselves on our blood. Those sleepless nights we sweated in bed next to each other beneath a single sheet, talking softly in the dark about a thousand things, about how certain we were of our special luck, of being different from everyone and everything we knew.

I remember the breeze that rescued us each night for a week in September. It blew in from Catalina, over the breakwater, and swept up the few short blocks from the harbor. It whispered through plants we'd potted on the balcony and wound its way into our living room. I remember the enormous eucalyptus outside our kitchen window swaying in the twilight. I remember the surprise of its million pink blossoms, which arrived one morning and stuck around for a month, maybe more.

I remember the first real meal we cooked on our new old stove. The two of us danced clumsily around each other with wooden spoon and steaming colander. I remember the scent of basil pungent on our fingertips and burning bread before breaking it.

And I remember dessert, a tart mango sorbet thawing on the counter as our bodies pressed into one another against the fridge. I remember the thrub of our fingers as they pushed through tiny magnets, parting clusters of silly poems left by friends and spilling them onto the floor. I remember us afterward, collapsed in our little kitchen, backs against the cool surface of lacquered cabinetry, the flesh of our bottoms on the linoleum, grinning under heavy eyelids as we picked up fallen words: *matter*, *simple*, *with*, *vision*, *almost*, *are*, *under*, *orange*, *euphony*.

Even now, I remember the sound of your voice when you asked me what that word meant: *euphony*. You said you hadn't heard it before. I said I was sure you had. Again you asked what it meant. But I asked you to repeat your question, begged you just to keep speaking. I wanted to make you understand the word the way I understood it. You asked a third time, then a fourth, then your voice lost its lilt. So I told you what I knew: it was something like harmony. Which reminded you of that tiny town up the coast we stopped into once. And with a laugh as bright as a ring of keys tossed into the air, you drifted back. Back to the fat white Maine Coon asleep behind the creamery window, back to the charm of an old red pickup rusting in tall grass. When you spoke, the lilt returned and lifted your voice like a dream. I hear it now still ringing in my ears.

3rd & Orange

~

*"Some day you'll come to Long Beach," she said.
"I will wait a long time, but you'll come."*

John Fante
Ask the Dust

3rd & Orange

It's the last night in June
and I'm on my way to a neighborhood bar
when I pass a man and a woman
perched in plastic armchairs
on the fenced-in lawn
of a run-down duplex

Side-by-side they booze
and curse each other's haggard faces
He exhausted
    Goddammit I told you she's just a friend
She frothing
    Just a friend Bullshit George
    I saw you suckin her tit at the back of the boat

A fisherman and his fishwife
souring in muddy porch light
      This is ugly truth

And yet
part of me wants to pull up a chair
or lean against their gate
and listen to them hash things out

But I keep my head down as I slip past
because I know enough to know
that whatever the rest of their story is

it doesn't belong to me
and I'm thankful to be so young
and untouched by sleaze
        forgetting for the moment
        I'm neither so young
        nor so untouched

At the bar
I copy their words onto the napkin
under my first beer
telling myself that at some point
somehow they will become useful

Several napkins later I pay up
and head back to my studio apartment
back down three blocks
through the gray-blue glow
of street lamps

I stop at my corner
the corner of 3rd and Orange
where behind the graffitied plexiglass
of a newspaper dispenser
Press-Telegram headlines
announce nothing I care to read about

For the world is now in the first hour
of the first day of another June
and once again

yesterday's news is old news
and I'm just waiting for the light to change

Overhead
a few faint stars glint
like tarnished sequins
tangled in night fog
that swirls in off the ocean
this time of year
and settles over this stuccoed neighborhood
of named and numbered streets

By the time the late-morning sun
finally burns away the last of this fog
I'll be a half-pot of coffee in
warming tortillas on an open flame
and scrambling eggs
to the familiar voices of weekend public radio

And I'll still have absolutely no idea that
in less than two months
I will meet you for the first time
and my life will change
in the most amazing
and unforgettable of ways

Neighbor

This is for Waco
who lives in the next building over

whose kitchen door opens
opposite my kitchen door
in the narrow passage that runs
between our two shoebox apartments

who smokes cigarettes down to the filter
or farther

who keeps more girlfriends than I do
and who salutes every passing woman
young or old good-looking or not
with a smile and a
     Hallo baybee
and is always saluted back

This is for Waco
who sings up to the windows of crying children
in the apartment above us
     Canta no llores

who was born and raised in Norway
and came for work in the harbor
who sailed with the Merchant Marines in WWII

and whose knotty forearms
bloom blots of indigo ink

who ambles with two canes
on legs as badly bowed as my grandfather's

whose face is furrowed from decades outdoors
but whose stub-fingered handshake
still clasps like a vise

who was the only neighbor to introduce himself first
when I first moved to this town

and who I sit with sometimes over coffee or beer
whose small company in this narrow passage keeps us
in conversation and laughter
which I will remember long after his time here is up
and I have moved on

It Begins Like This

The sky spreads itself completely
in a wide lonesome void
and beckons unbashful like a lover
neglected and needing
to be filled by another

And from there
        as always as ever
                out of the vast cobalt above
falls some delicate madman
howling happy throatmusic
        as off he drops tumbling down
appearing at first something like a speck
moving slow
                then
        slightlier in focus
like a wingshot bird whose arms flap
and flail
        and grab at wind
                in hope of flight or float

All along quickening thus
he plummets past scattered
clouds that dance rememberful
on tiptoes of sky-blue feet
billowing toward eternity beyond

But the funny thing is
       shit like this happens all the time

Stephen Crane Breakfasts
at Broadway Donuts

In the dessert
I saw a feature frosted oval
that filling the pastry round
spelled a tart at first glance
so I ate it

You said *Is it good, friend*

> *It is apple fritter* I answered
> *But I like it*
> *because it is fritter*
> *and because it's semi-tart*

Ambition

Preparing a trip to Bangkok
a good friend makes neat piles atop his bed
  pants shorts shirts
  socks underwear
  toiletries
  passport ticket printout

Across from him
I sit on the carpet
with my back against the lone armchair
sipping a can of Tecate
popping lime pulp
with my front teeth
as I flip through a book of ee cummings
he plans to take with him

  What do you think he says
and dumps two fistfuls
of colored condoms onto the bed
  Will I need all these

Looking up at him
I see how different we are
  Man I hope you'll need
  twothreefourfive times as many

This happy hope makes him smile wide
Jesus that would be a tall order
A tall order indeed

Then he stuffs
everything into a carry-on bag
for his red-eye flight
and we head out laughing
for a couple farewell schooners
at a bar up the street

The Aspiring Photographer
Reveals His Big Plan

I'm gonna take the perfect picture of a normal person
taking normal pictures of perfect people on perfect beaches
doing the perfectly normal things that perfect people on
perfect beaches normally do

Then he puts down the bong and adds
After that I'm gonna throw some cute little babies
in little cute clothes
and take some cute little pictures of them too

It'll be money

Oracle of the Open Heart

O what lovelies we spoke
glozing odic over not going home
or swooning for a young woman
a poet from school I know
who composed a poem
of one lone oval *O*
She called it *Love Letter*

And so it was so
Sole and solemn
she seemed to know

But lo
how foolish in our cups we grow
opining on stools about souls
about how thoroughly ours are shot
with lost lots and longings
that knock and crowd and hope
for another oneiric *O* of our own
another bold voweled vow of love
another fond promise not to soften
or become as the oath of youth
overgrown by doubt and old
but to go on hot and unbroken
as vapor from mouths in the cold

And so it is so

Afloat on booze another night flowed
onward for hours until we strode home alone
our pockets hollow our eyes low
poking holes in the truths of love we told
As if mortals could ever wholly know

For none knows more
than the Oracle of the Open Heart
She it is who discloses truth from the core
She it is who knows
our best and loveliest *O*s come so seldom
no words can totally unfold
just how voluptuously they flow
forthcoming like froth in honey
mountain sweet and moving slow

And She it is who honoring exposes
the holy heart of God and Love
how both lie wound around the same swollen symbol
of one absolute and extraordinary letter *O*

Orange & 3rd

~

He was like a pregnant woman, only that the thing inside him was not a baby but a youth. No, it wasn't a youth, it was a woman, young, and wearing a coat of mail like a knight.

Sherwood Anderson
Winesburg, Ohio

Write of Spring

Tonight I write of spring
and the all-day rain whose fall
whet a thirst for Friday night
the first in weeks free to drink our fill
and cut and thrust and chum
till last call we're out the door
with a couple easy-going gals
tramping and cheering and swearing
the Great Glory of Saturation
down a 4th Street full flood

Of spring pluperfect I write
of yesterday and last night
and this morning's snooze shaken by alarms
set for Saturday's midday box shift
that starts too soon at ten when
there is coffee and friends
and a simple scrambled breakfast
out a screen door that swings into sun
on a garden patio
and brick under bare feet
and never enough time to compose enough lines
in every woman's name and to revise
and revise until I get it right
until all my pages fill with praise
and light

Underdog

The Mexican dog is a mangy mutt
a mongrel eater of entrails
a half-breed licker of wounds and assholes
a loafer in parks and plazas
a loller in shade
a basker in light
always simple
and dreaming greedily of dirty things
       wet trash to nose around in
       fresh scraps to chew
       and the chase
       always the chase
       the sniffing and the humping
       always the humping

The Mexican dog is a hero
a sly barrio champion
where few are ever champion long

On a stuccoed wall in his neighborhood
there hangs a sign with his picture
       This dog can impregnate
       as many as seven bitches a day
The people have spoken
They want his balls on a platter
They want to bring him down

And yet any man who reads this
must shudder at such a sentence
and feel a pang of sadness
and a pang of envy
before he looks the other way

But it's always been like this
for the Mexican dog
who was *itzcuintli* once
the god-dog of death
lucky to be born
and bred to be eaten
by dark masters
who built their homes
in the great templed city on the lake
in the days before Cortez

And those days as these
this dog would sooner lift a leg on
as venerate a temple or its gods

For what are such things to dogs
but providers of half a day's cool shade
and just another place to piss

Bioluminescence

Just how we arrived
at pier's end
past midnight
cannot now be said
nor can memory tell
what we had in mind
walking out alone
but you followed
me up and over the gate
down the ramp
to the boat dock afloat
on the flat black water
lapping the pontoons
upon which we rose slowly
and slowly fell
breathing the briny night
where we sat
removed our shoes
rolled our pant legs up
swung our feet over
and slipped them
under the cold surface
as the sun-dried scurf of baitfish guts
crusting splintered planks
pressed our palms
and you

with your wild sound
rang and kicked the water
into a brilliance
into a million milky Tiffany lamps
shooting like stars scattering
across the muddled mirror of space
surfing out into a nothing
that made us spring
into something of our truer selves
part child part criminal
part ineffable cretin
just happy to splash
and splash until we realized
if it weren't for the hour
or the lack of towels
or change of clothes
or that I weren't the bolder
we could perhaps hazard a plunge
into that living galaxy lit below

The Sound of Swallowing

Sometimes the sound of swallowing you say
is so loud it's like thunder

How it rolls down the throat
How it rumbles in the ear

For hours together we stretch our goodnight
parked in my car near your place near the park
We sit and talk and wonder what we share
Could we outlast what brought and keeps us here
and what would it mean if we might

Face to face our eyes search the dark

Our lives are marvels hidden in plain sight
Will we blink or be bold in this chance to ignite
But all these questions end unmarked
when your kiss lands less like lightning
    more like a spark

Big Bang Theory

This is the way the world begins
This is the way the world begins
This is the way the world begins
not with a whimper but a bang

As orbits converge
our constellated skin collides
    kaBOOM
and countless freckles blur
in the birth of a new zodiac

We have overcome the gravity of other lovers

Let the universe choke on lightyears
We have no time for parsecs now

There shall be no astronomy
during the meteor shower

       only a sky of dazzling light
and the pulse of blood
like god and song

For ours is a new cosmography
ours the new Big Bang

Marginalia

My socks are off and my
feet are snug under your
butt between the cushion
of my couch where we
study
       But how can I
concentrate on textbooks
when the 17th century is
a dead past sad and stale
and colorless without you
The pages in this chapter
detail an age gone cold
an epoch out of which
you will never rise to pour a
glass of water from the sink
and lean against the frame
of a kitchen door in
unbuttoned blue jeans
long sleeves and ankle socks
and tilt your head to drink
as you did just now
       I fancy somehow a
day some little history may
gloss us too and so I make
this note in the margin
about the moment you

cup my face in your hands
and kiss the center of my head
and my eyes enclose their record
a vision of you I don't yet fear
to lose

       With your biology
book you resettle beside me
and I slip my feet back under
you and return to the
17th century where eventually
Julia and her Robert Herrick
compel me to a much deeper study
upon your magnetic beauty and
the comely curvature of your neck

Cigarettes and Coffee

It's two weeks until Christmas
and as cold as this town gets outside
when we step through the door
of my studio apartment

We're flush with drink
and back from dancing
to the songs of Neil Diamond
sung by Phil Shane
two names forever fastened to yours

In the kitchen
I pour us pints of tap water
turn on the oven
my poor fireplace
and lower down its door
to melt the chill that seeps
through warped wood-framed windows
and settles like winter around the room

I hand you your glass
which you clink against mine
and I turn the stereo on low
as we recall our conversation
with the older couple
we left dancing at the bar

How long did you tell them we'd been married

Five years I say
though we've hardly known each other a month

You think they believed us

I believed us

Me too you say
with a smile

It's late and we're tired
but wide awake sitting close
on the edge of my futon bed
listening to Otis Redding sing
    It's early in the morning
    about a quarter to three
    I'm sitting here talking with my baby
    over cigarettes and coffee now
    and to tell you that
    Darling I've been so satisfied
    honey since I've met you
and the song's saxophone
loosens something lodged within

Where have you been

You rest your head on my shoulder
and answer as in a dream
    Searching for you
    Searching everywhere for you

I don't know what else to do
but give thanks
    Thank you thank you god
    Thank you Mr Redding
and pray
    Please please
    Please be sweet
as our bodies buzz
and the room fills
with lush and drowsy heat

Waxing Moon

Tonight
the moon
looks the way
you make me feel

Just so
         happy and horny

On Unhurried Evenings Like This

On unhurried evenings like this
when clouds assemble in slabs
of dimpled slate and the sun's light
or what's left of it
shimmers to soften all it touches
I sense poems at the edge of everything
elusive and playful as a batch of
giggling young cousins dodging grown-ups
at a funny uncle's Thanksgiving get-together

So rare these evenings are
like catching strains of a
forgotten favorite song
as it slips from the window
of a passing car
on a quiet street

Full of tease and promise
they fall gently into your lap
like the exquisite head of a new lover

or like the first drops
of a rain in summer
which hover sneakily about the thick orange air
until you find them slowly seeping
through your short-sleeve shirt

wetting your face like tears
beading in the fine hair of your arms
sending warm welcome shivers
over your skin

Empiricism

To better hear the thick hush of your dark hair
I have my ears' pair

       Wrapped to the pulse of your each wrist
       these living hands form gentle fists

So wholly this nose the spice of your body charms
the back of your neck the inside of your arms

       And this my heart beats hard and best
       with my chest pressed against your chest

Too my eyes drink in the country of your thighs as
I savor everyplace above your belly below your waist

       And I hereby pledge my lips unto
       the very tips of your fingers and your toes

so that every bit of you
every bit of me better knows

Sprout

To become the word *sprout*
To sow my spirit in a syllable
sibilant and sounding out
To dispel death
with puckered plosive breath

To simply imply green
To evoke tendril life in you and youth
To fill your voice and hear it ring
To wisp within you infinitively
the tender promise of infinite spring

Morning Routine with Rain

Your body is a soft alarm
a murmur glowing warm
It gently wakes me with its call
as you push the covers back
to sit up against the wall
and yawn and stretch and blink

Outside raindrops plash and plink
Slowly cars part puddles with a splash
their motors purring as they pass

When the clock ticks quarter to six
at last you slip from bed to fix
coffee in the kitchen in bare feet
Then it's time to shower
after you feed the cat a treat

As I lay listening to you lather
I drift in half-dreams
of wet sounds and shower steam

Dressed and ready you come wake me
with a kiss good morning sweetly
and we whisper of the weekend
Saturday the farmers market
Sunday sailing with a friend

Then toast in one hand mug in the other
You head downstairs out the door

But I don't work till later
so I roll back over to snooze some more

After the Party

Tomorrow morning
after the party
long after everyone has gone home
after we have woken up late
and cleared the last glasses and bottles
from here and there
after slow cups of strong coffee
and a breakfast of hot waffles
after the morning has rolled itself
under the shade of another afternoon
we will lay down limb over limb
on the thick carpet of our living-room floor
and recall tonight's gathering of good friends
sitting cross-legged on the floor in rings
around the couch and chairs
their clusters and conversations
spilling into the hallway
their laughter
filling our kitchen with life

And when these memories begin to drift
      as memories do
to things that have gone before
back to the good pain of parents
and thoughts of older brothers
of all the dark and bitter beauty

humming in our blood
      I will stop
      and I will kiss your feet

And we will make us
      for an hour or so
forget about time

3rd & Junipero

~

In fervid hearts self-contained some brief experiences devour our human tissue as secret fire in a ship's hold consumes cotton in the bale.

Herman Melville
Moby Dick

Strike Everywhere

We're all searching
for that happy match

The one to light the fire that won't burn out

Returning at Dusk from a
Walk in the Hills

As I crunch
down this gravel
path back toward

the highway back
toward the car
that will carry

me home the
tenth month presses
cool shadows into

these brittle hills
and dusk cues
a chorus of

hidden crickets
whose song rises
like a fever

in low light
The way the wind
blows through this

dim canyon the
way the sycamores
silhouette against

the darkening sky
the smell of dirt
and sage and woodsmoke

from distant chimneys
The way all these
details gather and agree

it's begun again
to get later
         sooner

Balloon as Reminder

The droop
of a dying ballon

The slow
slow
         slowly deflating reminder of
some celebration

a birthday
or a birth

the passage of time

Heart Song

Birds gather in the garden at dawn
each possessed of its own native song
quilled in its heart like the streak of its wing

　　Such creatures have it easy whose lives are not long
　　who seldom die before they learn to sing

Dwelling

On mornings
coffee fails to stir the blood
the sizzle of a skillet
turns the stomach
and there is no warmth
in the light
through the kitchen window
nor news nor music
you care to hear
and everything comes too quick
or too loud or not at all
and the mind creaks
like feet on old wooden floors
with the unshakeable sense
something has been misplaced

      Mornings like these
long after you shave and shower
a shortness of breath
still clings to the chest

Shadow Play

Awake in a haze from a dream at dusk

> In the door the shape of someone to see you
> a face you have known a name you have lost
> in the sudden flush of black birds from a wire

But no

> All are just shadows moving on a wall
> cast by other lights some but cast most
> by the dark flicker of memory afire

Cold Snap

Shouldering through the door
we kick off wet shoes and
haul the groceries upstairs
into the kitchen in two trips
the damp bags bulge
about to burst in our arms

It's early January
and our day of errands is done
We peel off wet clothes
pull on dry socks
and crawl beneath our heaviest blankets
where we shiver like dogs

Outside the rain does not stop
and night like an icebox
closes in cold and dark

Half past eight a flash
        the neighbor's security lamp
We lift our heads
cancel plans for dinner
our voices half vapor

Then morning in the window
        a pale opal caught in frost

Coldest night since 1933
we learn later from a friend
who heard it on the news

But both were wrong

Colder nights were yet to come

Arsonist's Dream

These are not my woods
I wandered into them
on a side trail that broke
from the main path

This is not my land
but it is winter here too

These naked trees
brittle as twigs in the cold
their leaves scattered
across the forest floor

> All are dead brown and dry
> cracked like pages in old books
> or rimed with rot and black

> A scab of ice tops a pond

Finding a log along the track
I stop awhile to think and sit

I know not what to do with beauty
but burn it

Elm & 3rd

~

And after all these things
Is a question I must ask
When everyone has called me out
And said I am the worst
And asked for voices on my side,
My love, would you sing first?

Bonnie "Prince" Billy
"Three Questions"

Lily White

At a museum in Paris
you walked into an oval room
cool and white as a cloud
and found yourself surrounded
by Monet's last great obsession
   Water Lilies

You toured this room for a moment alone
strolling its circuit of canvas
absorbing its quiet color

But this was before I knew you
when you had shorter hair
and French filled your mouth
like a stranger's kiss

How I pictured your life then
with you in my arms
somewhere near sleep
as we talked of things we loved

There were lessons
I wished to learn
   What about these lilies was so special to you

You answered in a drowse

They were so calming and big
but about something so small

I lay and listened and closed my eyes
to a vision coming into view
      Life would open up again even wider
      and continue to

But we were spotless then
still spotless and new

Parting

You left in the late afternoon
your shoulders lush with summer light
the scent of pomegranate shampoo
full and fresh around your neck
      I was nearly ready to submit

On the curb I took your hand to say
But you took it back and went away

I should have called you back
tried to work things out
That we might was a thought
      Maybe we could
But the sound of your name
stuck in my throat
like splintered wood

I stood there dumb
and watched you go

Rounding the corner
at the end of the block
you looked back
But you were so far gone
Your expression had become
as inscrutable as a thumb

Was it at me you looked
or at the rising moon

This I wondered as I walked inside
where emptiness filled my room

After that we saw each other
once or twice more

It's hard to say for sure

After True and False

T or F: There are two sides to every coin

T or F: The ball is rolling

T or F: Change is a foot

T or F: Yesterday I was more tired when I woke than
　　　　when I went to sleep

T or F: You will craft an interesting life online

T or F: It is best to have the last word in an argument

T or F: Most days I carry less than nine dollars in my
　　　　wallet

T or F: Once in a while I smile for no particular
　　　　reason

T or F: I would rather be invisible for a day than fly
　　　　like a bird for two

T or F: Longing has a color and a flavor

T or F: I wash dishes by hand

T or F: I lack faith in machines

T or F: I miss certain people more than three times
　　　　a day

T or F: I cannot recall when I last saw her/him

T or F: I have begun to enjoy myself again

T or F: What others think of me can affect my
　　　　digestion

T or F: Already I remember certain things about you
　　　　forever

T or F: I have been disappointed by lovers

T or F: The moon is on the wane

T or F: Tonight I will lie down at a godly hour

T or F: Some of these statements and their answers
    may reveal something meaningful about me

T or F: None of this means shit

T or F: There is a ringing in my ears

T or F: I have significant regrets

T or F: I should cut out the drinking

T or F: This is one way of expressing gratitude

T or F: I see how this could become tedious

T or F: I will probably not cut out the drinking

T or F: I often prefer cooing and grunting to actual
    speech

T or F: Few individuals are really all that great

T or F: Who am I to criticize

T or F: He/She was on my mind when I last ate

T or F: We should have danced more often

T or F: I drove through butterflies to get to you

T or F: I am very fond of the way some people smell

T or F: Must I become a caterpillar again

T or F: I have been known to mishandle a
    compliment

T or F: When I was a child I had a toy or dream I will
    never forget

T or F: My memories are incandescent

T or F: This will collect dust or help fill a hole in the
    earth

T or F: Eventually there comes an end to all things

T or F: Drowning is acceptable

T or F: Looking handsome people in the eye can be tricky

T or F: I have yet to be completely honest about my own carnality

T or F: I am good at making bad decisions

T or F: This is not as exciting as it used to be

T or F: I become more likable as you get to know me

T or F: Some good news comes too soon

T or F: There are four or five things about me that would frighten my friends and family

T or F: The previous statement is a bit too heavy or a bit too dark

T or F: This reminds me of a poem I once read

T or F: Love

T or F: I hesitated before responding to the previous statement

T or F: One day I will collapse like a wooden shed in a field far off

T or F: I shall become like the yellow hills of California

T or F: I shall hold at least one secret sacred

T or F: This is complete horseshit

T or F: I have known hate

T or F: I could be tempted to kill if I were guaranteed to get away with it

T or F: I worry about my heart

T or F: If only I had studied harder

T or F: Some people deserve to have wild asses defile the graves of their ancestors

T or F: I should have been a pair of ragged claws
        scuttling across the floors of silent seas

T or F: Fuck that

T or F: Something better will come along

T or F: It is silly to take things so goddamn seriously

T or F: If I could feed a horse a Washington apple I
        might feel better

T or F: There was nothing about your body I didn't
        hold dear

T or F: Flesh and death are no match for me

T or F: I resent being given only two options

T or F: One of these days we will have lost all our
        chances

T or F: I will be reborn in rain

T or F: Most days I pay more attention to sunlight
        than politics

T or F: Sometimes I have more hands than I know
        what to do with

T or F: It is not likely we will end up with the person
        we most love

T or F: Would you please come home

T or F: This could be something unexpected and
        wonderful for some

T or F: I have been let down gently

T or F: Perhaps we should have waited longer

T or F: Is there something I can say or do

T or F: There will be more loneliness to sift through

T or F: If I had the chance I would do it all again
        with minor changes

T or F: At some point once will be enough
T or F: Some of my words will ring in your ears after
      we lose touch
T or F: Here goes

Dinner Guest

From the kitchen
the smell of good things cooking

      in the oven
      a pizza almost done

      the fragrance of homemade pesto

From another room
Your voice calls to me
clear and bright
      Dinner's on the table

Out of habit I almost answer

Sitting down to eat
I find your chair empty
the table bare

      I am alone in a strange house

Single Unit

In bed on my back
in the dark of a single unit
restlessness filters through walls

      Above the ceiling overhead
      television news
      and commercial breaks
      the scrape of a fork on a plate

Next door
a wracking cough
a struggle to breathe

      Across the hall
      a woman paces
      hushing in her kitchen
      the new baby's colic cry

Out the window
an alley of amplified night
the yawn of cars
under a full moon's long light

      In the futon's creak too
      the sound of absence
      breathing beside you

Envy

On the horizon
mountains white with snow
after a storm
      clear
      and clean
      and so close
you could reach out
and touch their bright crust

They think they know cold

I would crush them if I could

Father Son Portrait

In the foreground
my father and I

Behind us
sodden wooden fencing
the knotted branches
of a dormant cherry tree

It's the last morning of a short visit
Birds flit and chitter in the yard
and the sun lights a fire in a thousand dewdrops
as each with a hand in his pocket
slings an arm around the other's shoulder
and makes small talk
while posing for a picture
we can stick on the fridge

Just outside the frame
an idling car steams

Work Song

Whatever season it is
it is time

Shake the bitter months from your heart
Sweep the hardness from your mind
However you need to
        get it done

For even in the warmth
even while shines the sun
there's still work to do

There will never not be chores
and everyone must continue
and all must do their part
And yes you too
Even you must do yours

Whatever season it is it is time
        It is time
        It is time
        It is time

Pedagogy

Some days pass
with the slightest effort

We begin by doing something right
We walk into the room prepared
open with a small joke
or tell a little story
and from there everything flows

Where good humor leads the way
we do well to follow

Beating Heart Blues

What can be said of the heart
that hasn't already been said

What of its swell and sink and smart
What of its shape and hue and breadth

What can be said of the heart
that hasn't been already said
by some better one long since dead

Newborn

By spring god willing
a good friend's wife
will have their first baby
yet already he's writing
songs in baby's name
strumming them under stars
singing them like prayers

Though I know nothing
I have known him
long enough to see
somehow he will become better

And he needs to be
For when she arrives
in body as in name
everything will be everything

Nothing stays the same

Lone Ranger

Outside the market
a boy mounts a horse
sits astride its saddle
and kicks sun-stiff stirrups
of tooled leather

The horse of course
is just the hazel face of a machine-
sad stud fixed mid-leap
a fey fiberglass beast of burden
whose gloss has chipped

But the boy champs to begin
while Gramma
bow-legged and broad-backed
fishes quarters from her purse
to feed the slot
then trundles off
as the horse lurches
into a begrudging gallop
down its track of trumpets blaring
Hi Ho Silver Away

And the boy beams
caught up in the moment's movement

Unwatched he watches a scene unseen
He is not so old yet he can't still dream
of riding off into the sunset
of ditching Gramma
of leaving home and homework behind

Or maybe not
It doesn't really matter
No lope last forever

For the moment the boy is occupied
while Gramma visits the vending machine

But can you believe
an old horse like that here

It was the color of your eyes
I swear

Surface Tension

I doubt I was
the only one this morning
watching the rainwater bead
on our classroom window
Though from where I stood
I'm sure no one had
a better view

Beyond the pane
a row of swaying drip-darkened palms
Mirror-glass towers
silver in the downpour
The balance of another October

When
during small group discussions
there came a moment
so subtle and brief
no one noticed

      The voices of students
      whispered like traffic
      on Ocean below

Something eased
behind my eyes

inside my chest

A quiver ran through me
as if I'd drunk too much
although I'd drunk nothing for days

Suddenly I felt like singing

Atlantic & 3rd

~

I feel as if we opened a book about great ocean voyages
and found ourselves on a great ocean voyage

Tony Hoagland
"Voyage"

Sunken City

In a photograph
from a daytrip up the coast
you move still
against asphalt and ocean

For that brisk afternoon
the peninsula was ours
and we slipped under the fence
to walk those desert blocks
of broken street alone

Atop a tilted slab
you looked into my lens
and I captured you in full color
Through your hair streamed
all the splendor of the hour
and laughter lit your grin

Or was it just camera flare
caught in mist and wind

Writing Life

Some nights sing like giddy ballads
and print their melody in the mind
Some days run smooth as sonnets
impressing with their design
But morning begins in blank verse
It needs us to work the rhyme

Whether you build odes or epigrams
or layer epics line by line
may you lead your life like a pen in hand
and go on writing till you find
why or what you're living for
I wish you the best of luck and time

Agenda

☐ Ease into Sunday

☐ Visit book

☐ Make second pot of coffee

☐ Exercise at noon
with Garrison Keillor

☐ Shower and dress

☐ Take a walk
look around

☐ Think of brother

☐ Think of father

☐ Revisit book in the park

☐ Call mother

☐ Be a friend and
have a beer

                    (your days will not always be so easy)

☐ Start home at sunset

☐ Figure evening out
alone

☐ Iron work shirts and pants

☐ Wash dishes and clean up

☐ Go to bed

☐ Then back to work

☐ Next week
do it all over again

Phoenix Friend

You shivered
as flames engulfed you

You fell trembling
into your own ashes

I watched you die
trusting you'd return

that you'd remember the cycle
the way it works in life

how death comes for us again
and again

And so I stuck around
waiting where new life waits

to greet you when
your old life was done

So if you're ready now
open your eyes but slow

Let them adjust to the light
Everything will be be all right

Now dust yourself off
Step from your ruined nest

You must be thirsty
Let's walk and get a beer

Welcome back my friend
Cheers

Apartment Cleaning

I wake up
before the alarm
take a deep breath
and draw back the blinds

In the kitchen
I make coffee in the half-light

In the shower I give thanks for simple things
       hot running water
       the alchemy of percolation
       oatmeal and raisins
       decent teeth
       Sound and Vision

Then I make a sign to post outside

    MOVING SALE

    Futon bed
    Couch and Ottoman
    Chairs and Kitchen stuff
    Plates Mugs Glasses
    Utensils Pots and Pans
    Bed and Nightstand
    Desk and Lamp

Books and Shelves
Music and Stereo
Television DVD player
Dining table Coffee table

EVERYTHING MUST GO

Then I open my door and stand back
and wait for things to disappear

Around noon
a young couple wanders in
to look through records and books
As we chat
I fall quietly in love with them
But we're brief friends
heading in different directions
They carry Bill Withers
and Raymond Carver in their arms
out the door smiling and waving

When it's over
stuff that doesn't sell
goes into a box or bag
and into the alley
or down to the thrift store on 4th
where it can become someone else's belongings
another's boon or burden

And then comes time to clean

Through it all
I think of you but five times

>   picking up a bottle cap kicked to a corner
>   during the farewell party you weren't at

>   sweeping into a pile of dust
>   strands of long brown hair
>   beneath the bed I broke down

>   finding that striped sock you lost
>   and tossing it in the trash

>   hauling out the secondhand couch
>   we carried down Ocean
>   up Atlantic to complete our place

>   washing the tall windows in front
>   through which passed such pretty light

Then I think of you no more
I just sweep and mop the bare hardwood floors

After I pull the last nail from the walls
I spackle all the holes

forward

~

The story ends. It was written for several reasons.
Nine of them are secrets. The tenth is that one should never
cease considering human love, which remains grisly and
golden as ever, no matter what is tattooed upon
the warm tympanic page.

Donald Barthelme
"Rebecca"

Elsewhere

Somewhere there is a park lit up like gold at sunset
overlooking a city left behind

Somewhere behind clouds
is a sun you can stare straight into

Somewhere a kettle sputters on a stove
on a Saturday that lasts forever

where evening is poised above afternoon
like a story in a book on a bed face-down

Somewhere postcard bookmarks have all been sent
or lost or laid to rest in an old shoebox

Somewhere friends at the end of the bar
invite a stranger to share their pitcher of beer

and a pier runs out over waves where
fishermen fiddle with tackle as talk turns to travel

Somewhere a train heads downtown
while a boat sails past the breakwater

and people meander through farmers markets
as swimmers cross the bay

Somewhere the musk of earth is released by rain
and lithe legs open their warm welcome

Somewhere a song is mistaken for an old friend
while windows are raised and doors propped open

for company and cold drinks that glimmer
on a balcony strung with lights

where a table is spread full as the summer night
Somewhere a backyard bursts with dahlias

as a hundred giant kites hover above a beach
and holidays fall back in line

Somewhere monarchs dream of Mexican hills
as a wind stirs the dust of another autumn world

where hearts still flutter and
freckles are counted with thanksgiving kisses

and a Christmas tree is tied down
for a rooftop ride home

to a new front room where candles are lit
and speech fails the press of lips

in a bedroom where shoes and socks slip off
ahead of the laying on of hands

and vows made are kept
like boots ready for the trail

Somewhere it is almost time to go
but not too late to turn back

as we reach the middle of our short storied lives
far from their beginning uncertain of their ending

Somewhere dreams do not die at dawn
and everything essential remains

Somewhere a dog frisks in circles
to the lift of its leash from a hook by the door

and a plane departs for the trip
Somewhere pain is overpowered

as delight filters through cracks
as friends carve pumpkins to perfect playlists

on newspaper floors
Somewhere bartenders still recognize the faces

whose names they never knew
as whales swim down the coast

toward Baja lagoons
Somewhere a hot bath is filled for a tired lover

and winter sweeps in with the fallen leaf
as a belly begins to swell

and plans are finally hatching wings
Somewhere a coffee shop door swings open

and the sound of bells
sparkle like the harbor washed in light

that flows over the peninsula
lambent as creamed honey

as the town turns on again
shimmering with good news

Somewhere prophecies are fulfilled
or brushed aside in favor of food with friends

around a bench in the park
Somewhere a single-screen theatre dims

as curtains rise and the movie begins
Somewhere a couple finds each other

dancing in a living room above a street
where hearts don't outgrow each other

or falter on fickle fuel
and the trick of the new doesn't wear off

with every cool breeze that blows down the block
Somewhere the idea of death loses its pall

as another numinous word is learned
that will transform the world by saving a soul

Somewhere there will be an awakening in darkness
where no evil indecision crawls

and morning will land light on eyes
that open for one last look around

before the musician picks up his guitar
and quibbling questions can be safely forgotten

and worries swapped for a nap in the grass
as time and place unravel

and what once was together comes apart
to take form anew further along

Because somewhere there is a garden blooming
in a valley after a season of health

in a town under a sky whose blue is just a color
calm and quiet as ever

And somehow we will have made it there
only to find ourselves missing somewhere else

afterward

~

*A naked man with a startled look who has been
to history and back.*

Aimee Bender
"The Rememberer"

I

My first night in Long Beach was a good one. I'd spent the day at my father's house packing up boxes in an old room and moving them to my new studio apartment. Late in the afternoon, a friend came by with his van to help haul whatever wouldn't fit in my car. The sun flared in the windshield as we drove through traffic on the 605 toward the ocean.

It was dark by the time we got everything inside. Cold beer was our reward. We cracked the first round in the kitchen, lifted tall cans to new beginnings. The room was all white walls and jumbled boxes. The first thing I did was hook up my stereo. What we listened to I can't recall and what we talked about I can't remember. But we talked and laughed and listened to music as I went about removing things from boxes. Later, we stood bullshitting on the street, sharing a cigarette before he drove off.

Back inside, I was alone. But I felt no creeping fear. I felt no anxiety or confusion about what to do next. My new place was maybe 400 square feet, a shoebox of an apartment. But to me it felt amazingly spacious and full of potential.

I finished the last of my beer and made my bed. A slight buzz made my already dazzling optimism electric. It had been a long day and I hummed with the unmistakable sense that I was on the cusp of fantastic new experiences. A new adventure had begun. Unforeseen opportunities would soon reveal themselves. Great discoveries awaited me. There were fascinating new neighbors to meet, whole new neighborhoods to explore, streets and blocks and routes to learn. I turned out the lights and laid myself down in the tingling dark. Behind my blinds, a security light in the courtyard shone soft and confident. I closed my eyes and wondered what untold brightness the future held for me here.

That first night I dreamt only good dreams, and woke refreshed. I opened my blinds to let in the light. A grand new day! I put some music on. I stepped into a hot shower. So what that I didn't have a shower curtain? I had a closet of fresh clothes and plenty of time to cook and eat breakfast before work.

Outside, the morning was crisp and clean. In the breeze, the glorious tang of the sea. In my mind, the freshness of all fresh things. I walked up the street to my car, my eyes roving over the buildings where my neighbors lived. I felt a new appreciation for stucco. Beneath my feet, the sidewalk split in patterns delicate as lacework. And here was rosemary, fragrant in a planter. I took note: someday soon I would pinch a sprig to make some bread. I would learn to bake. I twirled my keys and a thought came to me: *The world is a flower unfurling.* The words played in me as I approached my car, where, tucked under the wiper, was a neat white envelope. Could it be—a love letter already? I lifted the wiper and plucked it out. Inside: a ticket from the streetsweeper: a $50 fine.

This was the morning of Thursday, January 15th, 2003. The next morning a second streetsweeping ticket was waiting for me.

Those early days I was a goddamned dreaming fool.

＿

Over the next ten years I collected lots of parking tickets. Every so often I was moved to write a letter to the city. In my first, I sought mercy and told the truth: I was brand-new to the neighborhood, hadn't noticed the signs or even expected them. There'd been no such thing as citations or fines for street sweeping in my last neighborhood. This was true, and the letter succeeded: my two back-to-back tickets were dismissed. Compassion and decent-mindedness were not dead.

But the tickets kept coming. Later letters included checks along with polite suggestions for reforms. Maybe residents could keep their $50—or have their fines reduced—if they immediately swept where their car had been? Where was the harm in this if, in the end, the sweeping got done? Sometimes I appealed a ticket on the basis of extenuating circumstances. No sign had been posted—it'd been ripped out of the ground—its hours and days had been obscured by graffiti, stickered over. Surely an exception could be made—I had worked two shifts that day, stayed late at school studying in the library, been too exhausted to drive around hunting for the single open parking space three blocks away where the sweeper came at 3am and I worked again at 4am. I needed rest. And it wasn't safe to walk so far so late at night in my neighborhood. In the rain. With a sprained ankle. And the flu.

I wrote what I thought would yield mercy. Did I exaggerate? The fines were a financial hardship. And my despair in the moment of composition was honest, my ethics pristine.

As the fines increased, so did my conviction that the city's parking restrictions were designed to prey on its working-class neighborhoods. Mine was a simple theory: unscrupulous city planners in cahoots with greedy property developers lined their pockets with fines paid by people who found it easier to submit to the city's petty vampirism than sue for change. In this way I fed my indignation.

Eventually the tickets came less often. And when they did, I just mailed a check.

My last street-sweeping letter to the city is dated January 13th, 2013. I typed it sitting on the hardwood floor of my last apartment, my back against a wall. It was written in a burst of weary zeal, its tone sharpened to prick the conscience of whatever paper-pusher picked it up. As far as I can tell, this letter was promptly ignored. But I expected as much. Writing it was just a way of screaming into the void, and I was due for a good scream.

I'd recently gone through an ugly break-up. The affair had been brief but intense and left me sickened. I felt like I'd been poisoned. I was full of cold fire. For a time, all I could do was watch it rage. When I sat down to write the city, the blaze had died down, but the damage was done. From the smolder and ruin came the sound of a small voice I recognized, asking myself: *What the fuck had happened?*

It's not that the short relationship had meant nothing. It just hadn't meant much. Most painful by far was the way its failure inflamed the memory of another, earlier relationship, one I thought I had reckoned with but knew I hadn't. What made everything worse was the creeping realization that, if I wanted to save myself, I was going to have to make some big changes. I had to cut ties with the city, my sense of home and community, and the comforts of the life I'd made for myself. I was transfixed with shame and terror.

Eventually I dragged myself back from the brink of self-pity. I felt a powerful need to scream, to re-assert a sense of myself that had atrophied. So I chose a void slightly less abstract: Long Beach City Parking Enforcement. I needed a vent for the anger and disappointment I'd accumulated over the previous decade, even though I knew most of it, like the parking citations themselves, was nobody's fault but my own. And writing a last salty letter provided a welcome distraction.

In two days, I would leave Southern California. I didn't know when or how I'd return or where I'd go when I did. I had just cleaned out my apartment and gotten rid of most of my stuff in a weekend-long moving sale. What was left I donated to the thrift store or stored in a friend's garage until I could come back for it. I was still mourning, but the purge helped lighten my mood. I was approaching the end of what I understood would be the Long Beach chapter of my life. And I was eager to turn the page.

All of which meant, it was high time to let the petty collectors of parking fines have one last piece of my mind. This would be the last check of mine they'd ever cash. And who knew? Some faceless, forlorn individual trapped at a desk in a department cubicle might even, on some primal level, be cheered by the act. It felt good to imagine the possibility.

II

Ten years earlier, newly arrived in Long Beach, I had no idea how many parking tickets I'd rack up, how many hundreds of dollars I'd eventually burn on fines. How could I? I had no clue I'd stick around as long as I did. I was barely 23. I could hardly make out the shape of the weeks and months directly ahead of me. My only definite long-term plan was to transfer to Cal State before the year was up, which left plenty of time to figure out how that process worked.

In the meantime, there was work and rent. Rent was $525 a month, twice what I'd paid for a room in a house with three roommates only two years before. Work was part-time, three or four days a week at Trader Joe's, where the pay wasn't bad but wasn't great either. I was afraid another ticket could screw my ability to make rent on-time. Instead of working out a budget or picking up extra hours at the grocery store, I found a second job.

I also enrolled in classes at Long Beach City College. I didn't need any more classes to transfer. But I took a few to keep busy as well as to prove something to myself. I had enrolled at LBCC once before, fresh out of high school. I lasted a month before I withdrew. *Intro to Astronomy* and *Metal Working 1: Jewelry* were too much for me. I was out of my league, an interloper. It's a funny story now, but at the time the experience left me feeling pathetic.

My life is filled with these kinds of stories. Most can't be rewritten. But I thought it would be worth trying with this one. So much time had passed. I had grown.

A year after I graduated high school my parents split up. Like so many similar stories, the story of their unraveling is as complicated as it is unexceptional. And though the announcement seemed to come out of nowhere, a small part of me half-expected it. Most of my friends' parents had gotten divorced years before, and there were signs that things in our home had been slowly falling apart for a while. When my mother moved out the collapse was complete.

Before she left Southern California, my mother gave me a present of a small gold ring. I recognized it immediately as her father's wedding band. As a kid, I'd tried it on many times, but it was always too large for even my thickest finger. It fit perfectly now.

From then on, I wore that ring every day. It became a sort of talisman. My finger felt funny without it. Whenever I took it off, it went into a tiny box on my shelf. Sometimes a day might pass before I noticed I wasn't wearing it, and I would panic thinking I'd lost it. After a frantic search, it always turned up—in its tiny box, caught in my bedsheets, or left in the pocket of a pair of jeans I'd tossed into the hamper. But until I found it again my mind was never quite right.

Some people have no problem remaining in the town where they grew up. This was not the case for me. In Downey, even before my parents split up, everywhere I turned reminded me of failure. I had to get out.

A friend of mine had done it. She worked and saved for a year or two after high school. Then one day she was living in the Bay Area, 450 miles away. Such things were possible. But she was braver than me.

I went to Long Beach. Fifteen miles was a less intimidating leap, and it landed me next to the water. Though its downtown was small, Long Beach felt like a real city. It had an air of history. It didn't feel like the dead-end Downey did.

I went to Long Beach because it was close and because it was familiar. My father had gone to college there on the GI Bill. My mother had lived there when she and my father started dating. I was born there. As a kid, I swam at Mother's Beach and ate at my parents' favorite old burger joint, long gone from 2nd Street. I hunted crabs with my brother down on the rocks near the Queen Mary while my grandpa fished and drank beer nearby. After high school, I went to parties at coworkers' apartments and to visit my older brother during his first hopeful stays in sober-living houses on Ocean and 7th Street.

There was also the matter of college. Few in my circle of friends were doing the college thing. But this wasn't a problem. Following high school, most of us slipped easily into idleness. We spun our wheels in part-time jobs and gym routines, music and house parties and teetering romances we thought might save us. We drifted along, enjoying ourselves. We trusted clarity of purpose would come our way. In the meantime, I chipped away at general education requirements with the vague idea that I would eventually collect enough units to transfer to a four-year school and complete a degree. But I had doubts about college. And I was at least as aimless as anyone in my group, maybe more.

At the time, I had in my head the idea that I would become a writer. It seemed simple enough and somehow right. I didn't know what else to do.

But how serious was I? After all, real writers wrote and I hardly wrote much. I kept shitty journals. I wrote long letters and emails, filled the backs of postcards. I wrote essays in school. Did these count? I wrote poems in my room. Lots of bad poems. But I worked at them, trying to get better. Sometimes I thought I detected improvement. Most of the time I was just polishing turds. Occasionally I tried writing a short story. A couple pages in, I'd throw up my hands in frustration. All my beginnings resisted their endings and I hated them for their stubbornness. But I was stubborn too, and desperate to put something worthwhile on a page.

I had no shortage of ideas. They came freely and continuously. I filled Post-Its and cocktail napkins with them. Ideas stained the back of my left hand like crummy tattoos. They ran crazily up and down receipt paper, whatever was handy. A certain phrase or an image could send me into a fervor. Who knew whether one of these ideas might grow into something great? Scraps I'd scribbled on fluttered from my desk every time I opened a door or window. Ideas and false starts cluttered until they were crumpled and tossed into the trash.

Was this how one became a writer? I had no clue. I

lacked a model. I hadn't known any writers growing up, and I didn't know any serious readers aside from my brother and parents. If I received any guidance in school, it wasn't much more than the general encouragement of a couple English teachers. The only writers I knew were those of books I read. But they only showed me what *could* be done, not *how* one actually did it.

Because I wanted to write, I decided to major in English. I figured studying literature would expose me to great writers and thinkers from whom, with the help of my professors, I'd learn the ropes. I'd come out the other side of college a writer, with a degree to boot. All without having to take another math class. It made great sense to me.

I gave very little thought to other options. The fine arts were completely out of the question—I had no talent for them. Nor did I have the patience for the sciences or a mind for math. I didn't want to follow my parents into healthcare and I had zero interest in running a business. Money was nice, but I'd seen how busy and distracted my parents had been, and that made me distrust "stable" careers. The social sciences mostly bored me. History was more exciting, but I was drawn to literature. It was the one subject in school whose work brought any joy or consistently held my interest.

Majoring in English seemed as good a path or better

than any other in front of me. With time and experience I might even learn to write something worthwhile.

Was I crazy? I couldn't tell.

III

I trusted that good writing would come looking for me. It would find me because it knew where I lived. It would recognize me by my golden ring and know what had to happen. It would understand what sort of fool I was, and that I needed it to play nice.

And sometimes it came and played nice. Poems, like little miracles, bestowed themselves on me whole. *Whole!* Were they any good? *Who cared!* They had come to *me*, chosen *me—they were mine!* They came to me as I rode my bike to school and work, walked the halls between classes, searched for a title in the library stacks, lifted crates of milk, stocked shelves with canned food, rang up customers at the checkout stand, fixed breakfast and made dinner. At all hours, dark or light, words and ideas came. The brilliant arc of a story or some fulsome final scene would shoot through me out of nowhere. Sometimes only a line or two would come, maybe a single phrase. But the way they jumped in me, so sweet and willing, I knew their friends would come dancing along, arms outstretched, radiant, and I would sweep them up and take them home.

Within me was great promise! This thundering thought alone was enough to console me. How many countless good ideas I carried to the page, ideas for stories so powerful they would make readers weep, so ardent they would sear the soul of anyone who picked them up. One or two would, I was sure of it, melt mens' minds. If only I could find the time to sit down and write. I pedaled harder, drove faster to get home.

But when the fever passed and I read back over what I'd written... *my god!* Whatever had glowed or gloated in me now groaned and growled. I cringed at my own ridiculousness. This was *writhing* not writing. What the hell had happened? Had I not gotten home quick enough? Had I not written fast enough? Why couldn't I transfer my promise to the page?

So many good ideas teased me, then turned their backs and walked away. So I let them go. And good riddance! The little shits could get some other schmuck to do their work. They hadn't been worth the effort anyway. They weren't half as good as I thought.

So it went. Every now and then, I got so fed up I quit writing altogether. I just refused to do it. Days would go by and I'd ignore my head, dismiss every silly impulse and let the ideas pass on by, on their way to the next chump in line. Fuck 'em. Such an attitude made me feel generous, carefree. I was in control. My hands and mind could be put to better use. But when this superior feeling ran out, I was back at it, furious, scribbling on scraps of paper, writing on the back of my hand, in a notebook, opening new computer files. That most of the ideas would be abandoned or lost didn't matter. I was giving in to compulsion. And as long as I kept storing up ideas, I didn't have to sit down and sweat over developing them.

I clung to the idea that writing was something that would just happen, gradually or in a burst. Any day a great idea could occur, and as long as I was ready, all I needed was to sit back and channel it, let it flow, let it speak through me. In anticipation, I kept paper and pen handy. Computers couldn't be trusted. But how to turn the good idea into something more after it arrived? I knew it could be done because I'd done it myself a few times. But I was becoming afraid of the work it took. Ideas had a way of starting as such buoyant, weightless things. Why did they always have to become so damn heavy?

I dug my heels in. I told myself stupid things like *Somehow the work will work itself out.* I was unwilling to concede the point to virtually every real writer I'd read on the subject—unwilling even to learn from my own experience—that *the writing was the work.* But I rejected the burden of this simple truth along with another: If I wanted to get more work done, wouldn't it be best to approach writing with some methodical plan, like a schedule? *Maybe.* But schedules meant work, and work meant drudgery, and did I really want to write if it had to be like that? I was on too much of a schedule already. I was busy living. I worked. I went to school. I had bills to pay, dishes in the sink. My bathtub needed scrubbing. And the sun was so pretty. The rain so inviting. There was a world to explore. And wouldn't my mother appreciate a call? And what about my brother?—*I must consider the plight of my brother.* In my daily rounds, it seemed all things were infinitely more pressing or pleasant than a confrontation with words and beginnings that bloated in the mind only to die on the page.

So why make myself crazy? Why allow things to get so desperate? Maybe it was best to take it easy, stop trying to force things. I could coast along fine just storing up ideas. So that's what I did.

As an English major, I wrote a lot for school. In the margins of my papers, my professors drilled into me the values of clarity, relevance, detail, organization, elaboration and support. Their feedback helped me grow. But I could feel a stiff formality creeping in. It strangled the life out of my sentences, poisoned them with pretension.

I wanted a voice that *sang.* I wanted to ring out like Whitman, Cummings, and Millay. I wanted to impress like Nabokov, Cheever, and Ondaatje. I wanted to charm like Carver, Barthelme, and Bender. I wanted their grace and humor and wisdom. Something in me responded powerfully to these writers. How could I train to do as they did?

This question led me to creative writing classes. In these spaces I sat with others like me, all of us struggling to bring to the page something worth reading. We read each other's work, witnessed each other's failures, and critiqued each other's successes. This was helpful and the classes gave me a good excuse to produce. Having an audience and deadlines was both terrifying and exhilarating, and I needed the jolt.

I submitted some poems to the campus literary journal. Their acceptance, my first, left me high for a week. At the encouragement of a classmate, I got involved with the campus newspaper and wrote a few things for it. After finishing my degree, the confidence these experiences gave me sent me in search of opportunities to write for local publications.

Around this time, a small weekly newspaper appeared in Long Beach. Though a distant memory now, at that time everyone I knew read it. We read it in the break room at work, at the local coffee shop, at home on the couch. I sent its editors an email and, to my surprise, got invited to one of their writers' meetings. I was given an assignment. Then I was given more. Then I placed a few stories with other publications. Most of these pieces were short, but I was proud of them, and they all paid. The checks were small in the grand scheme of things. Most important was that I felt I had finally earned the right to call myself a *writer.*

＿

And I still call myself a writer, although it hardly

matters much.

Unless the things you write can be purchased in an actual bookstore or read on a website of someone else's design, calling yourself a "writer" is sort of like sharing that you have HPV or a special fondness for your own flatulence. It's a risky, slightly shameful divulgence, and usually more than a bit repulsive to most decent-minded people. Worse, it's utterly common.

Yet here I am. And writing is still hard to do well. Or quickly. Or at all. It's odd. Sometimes I wonder if I'd be in a better place now if I had followed a different path then. Sometimes I wish I had.

What I mean by this is that I'm also a teacher these days, and something in me can't help but want to be a lesson. So I imagine a scenario that pleases me: Maybe a reader, a student, a writer—someone like me struggling somewhere down the line—will come upon these words and recognize the sympathy that exists between us. Maybe this reader will feel slightly less alone. Maybe this recognition will be a comfort, an encouragment. Or maybe they will take heed.

Sometimes I wish I could get rid of my desire to write. But I don't know how I would. I'm not sure desire works like that.

~

It seems to me that many who express a desire to write—or pursue some other creative path—find it easier to drink beer, dream, loaf, despair, read, and talk shit. That is, they find it easier to do almost anything other than the work creativity requires. I know this because I'm one of them, and I've met plenty others like me along the way. But there are some among us who seem able to manage it all—write, make music, paint, teach, build things, drink beer, work a respectable job, raise a family, stay fit, stay social. While in Long Beach, I was lucky to develop friendships with a few in both groups.

One of these friends I used to meet for coffee at Broadway Donuts on days I didn't have class or worked a late shift. We liked the older couple who ran the place. They weren't much for small talk but they had decent coffee at a decent price and made the best apple fritters.

Because there was nowhere to sit inside their tiny shop, we sat outside. In plastic chairs we talked about books and music, the news, anything that entered our heads as the shop's door swung open and closed and people came and went. Sometimes someone we knew would stop and chat and sip their coffee with us. When old timers in the neighborhood came around with their dogs, we bullshitted with them too. Across the street in the 7-11 parking lot, some poor bastard already stumbling drunk or high would holler and make a scene. Cars rolled past with stereos so loud they made your eyeballs rattle. Now and then a woman, stunning in the morning light, would glide past, and curve the topic of conversation for a moment.

On mornings we had time, we'd shuffle over to a nearby café to take advantage of their dollar breakfast: two eggs, two strips of bacon, and two triangles of buttered Bimbo toast for one cash dollar. Frugality was a challenge we mutually embraced.

Since we lived only a couple blocks from each other, in the evenings we'd meet at one of our apartments to share a meal and listen to music. He was a musician and made a habit of writing songs, all of which were good, some of which were great. Sometimes he took up his guitar and played.

It helped that we both liked beer. At our neighborhood bar, we'd sit and talk over $5 liters of pale ale, one of the last best deals on drinks I ever saw. He had a special genius for plucking ideas for stories and poems from our rambling conversations. He saw creative opportunities almost everywhere he looked. *That's a good idea for a short story,* he'd say. And it would be. *You should write a poem about that.* And I knew I should. Over a game of pool, he'd begin with a *What if,* and together we'd spin out the idea until it was practically written. But most of these ideas were lost on the walk home. The rest dissipated during the next day's 4am shift at the grocery store, or evaporated while I worked on an essay for school.

Developing a writing habit was hard, so I developed a

reading habit instead. Of all the possible habits I might pick up, reading seemed about the best. As a student of literature, reading was a pleasure and a duty. I had centuries' worth of gaps great and small to fill. I misunderstood so much.

On campus one day, I fell into a conversation with a couple classmates, all of us English majors. A question was raised: Why had we chosen our major? One said he'd chosen it because he needed a degree to enter the military as an officer, and figured creative writing would be the easiest path. The other's father had promised him a position in the family contracting business as long as his son got a degree—*any* degree—and English seemed the quickest path. My stomach turned. I'd chosen the major because I loved reading and writing. But my path hadn't been quick or easy. I'd chosen literature because I was searching for a better direction to point my life. I thought maybe I could find it in good books.

If my explanation sounded precious then, it makes me shiver now. And yet in that moment it was one of the most earnest things out of my mouth in months. I was totally sincere: I truly believed I might somehow be saved by a story.

Such a faith in literature has become a recurring source of embarrassment for me.

Every gap I filled with books only exposed more gaps. I wanted wisdom and came away with words. Even then I knew the salvation I needed would take more than books. What I needed had to come from within. It had to spring from the action of my life itself. Only a damned fool would think otherwise.

IV

I worked at Trader Joe's for eight years. During that time, I dreamt of John Updike's A&P grocery clerks. I dreamt of Studs Terkel's box boy. I dreamt of William Eggleston's cart-pusher, dapper in his apron, collared shirt and tie. I dreamt of what I could do to help dignify the American grocery worker, a character so familiar, relatable, and full of dramatic potential. Markets were a rich and timeless setting.

But what would be my plot?

Between customers, I made notes on register paper whenever some interaction suggested humor, intrigue or insight. Arranging apples and oranges, onions and potatoes, I sketched scenes set in the produce aisle. In the stock room, to the sound of the hydraulic box-crusher, I cribbed from my co-workers dialogue more interesting than I could invent. I winced whenever one of these promising sketches turned up as mulch, forgotten deep in the pocket of pants I'd put through the wash.

For a time, I collected customers' discarded grocery lists. I envisioned a ground-breaking project: the first epic poem of the grocery store. It would be a mammoth undertaking, kaleidoscopic, documentary, collaborative. I enlisted my co-workers' help. A thousand years in the future, our work to preserve and contextualize such ephemera would provide researchers unique and valuable insights into the cultural and dietary habits of Southern Californians in the earliest years of the 21st century. Exactly how to frame such a work required special attention. But when I figured that out, something great and original would surely emerge. The problem played in my mind as I gathered carts, stocked shelves, checked and bagged groceries. The hunt was on.

Most of these lists were on Post-Its. A few were on real-estate brokers' freebie notepads. Some were written in large, looping letters, others in elegant script or chicken scratch, and one or two in the shaky handwriting of the infirm. A couple were typed. One had been drawn up on a computer spreadsheet, with headings and subheadings. Doodles and marginalia accompanied reminders not to forget *Brocoly?, Cat Cookies, Brie Cheese, toffuti, NFmilk, Tamales, ½ & ½, Everything Crackers, Pet BBQ, vino blanco, rutabagas, puff booty, snack food item, mostacciolli, woman essential oil, Poopie's diapers, Poopie's ice creamie, paper goods!, Morningstar bacon, Simple green,* and *moo moo food.* What did it matter that TJ's never sold rutabagas, mostacciolli or diapers? This was pure poetry! There were real human stories here.

The collection yielded other finds. One was a hand-drawn map of North and South America, bulging and unrecognizable if not for the names of a few principal cities. On its flipside, someone had written clumsily but scathingly: *Now matter where he goes, he always finds problems. Now matter how long she studies in collage, her knowleidge doesn't grow. No matter who they ask, they can't find information.*

The message stung as if it were addressed to me.

As the weeks went on, my vision for the project morphed into something less distinct and more challenging. Another angle of approach was needed. Maybe it was best to let the whole thing marinate awhile before returning to it. I filed the lists away, another project abandoned, and likely for the better. But who can really say?

One evening on a bike ride home from work, I stopped off for a pint at a 2nd Street bar. It was midweek, mid-May, and my first year at Cal State was now behind me. I sat alone at the bar, at peace, reading. But after a few pages, I became so distracted by the music I had to put my book down to listen. It was unspeakably stunning, revelatory. What was it? *Astral Weeks,* the bartender said. I made a note on my hand.

What was I doing with myself? What was the action of my life? I was blessed but idle, biding my time but lacking any larger plan. I believed it was enough to just go to work and school, to just pay better attention to beauty as I read in the grass or swam in the ocean or strolled the streets.

Were these not valid ways to find oneself? Were these not valid ways to fall in love?

～

Cashiering early one Sunday afternoon, I remember I was happy. It was late summer. I was singing along to The Beatles on the store stereo. I had half an hour to go till the end of my shift. I had plans to cook dinner with friends. The lines at check-out were eight carts deep. The store was swollen with families, hungover couples, and Leisure World retirees. I was doing my thing, greeting customers, asking if they'd found everything okay, making small talk as I bagged their groceries and bid them farewell. Life was bouncing along.

At some point I looked up to notice a young woman step into my line. She was smiling and singing too and moving closer with each customer I sent out the door. Soon we were standing in front of each other, I was taking the basket she was handing me, her vegetables were being rung up. There was a light in her eyes. We spoke. Maybe we said something about The Beatles. Maybe I praised George Harrison, the fresh weather, her patience, her smile, her freckles, whatever—I was full of praise. It bubbled in me like spring water. Then I was putting her bag in her hands. Our entire interaction couldn't have lasted much more than 3 minutes. And I never asked her name. Later that evening, in the kitchen with friends, I was still standing in front of her.

Two weeks later, a new semester had started and I was coming from the library to work a rare overnight shift. I walked in through the sliding doors just before closing time and my heart jumped when I saw she was one of the last customers in the store. I had hoped to see her again, and now she was even more beautiful than I remembered. In her hands was a bouquet of cut flowers. A co-worker rang her up—I hovered close, blushing, giddy, grasping for words that wouldn't come the way they had before. I was a fool.

When my shift finished at 3am, I walked out to my car and found, under my windshield wiper, yet another parking ticket.

But this was no ticket. It was a handwritten invitation: *Would I like to meet for coffee sometime?* At the bottom—a name and number. She'd been looking for me too.

I drove home in a swoon through empty streets. Every light was green.

Our first date was a friendly affair. I picked her up at her place. She introduced me to a tortoise and her cat. For support I brought along a buddy of mine and she brought along her roommates and together we drove to a record store in Hollywood. We were in high spirits. Our friends helped keep us in lively banter, and we laughed the whole way there.

At the record store, we roamed in a loose group

through the Rock & Pop aisles, lifting albums and artists from the bins, extolling, agreeing, guffawing—all the time signaling what we loved in life. I found a used copy of the album I wanted. We went for Thai food. The conversation, like the entire evening, continued to flow.

On the way back, the freeway was clear and the night was warm. In the backseat our friends were still laughing, but we were quieting down. I put on the CD I bought. The music had been on my mind for months. That night it was even more beautiful than I remembered. By the end of the third track, her hand was in mine. Her touch was unspeakably stunning, revelatory.

However we had arrived at this moment, whatever choices I had made, whatever turns she had taken—good, bad or otherwise—none of them mattered now. What could they possibly have to do with *us?* Not a damn thing. Nothing at all. We would lean in to love. We were the people we had been waiting for.

And like *that*, a decade's worth of drift, the slog of another semester, the ungodliness of another 4am shift, all shame and gloom began to evaporate. I began filling up with a confidence and contentment I'd never known.

—

She was a dancer and we fell easily into rhythm together. Within weeks we were hatching plans to travel. Within months we were boarding a plane. Within the year I finished my degree and we were moving in together. These were big steps, leaps of faith, firsts for both of us. But they felt natural and right. This was the first serious relationship I'd had with someone who hadn't known me since middle school. She was like no one I'd ever met. And she loved with such terrific brightness. She inspired me to become something new—an upgraded version of myself.

In this way something far better than any poem or story found me.

V

The vast majority of individuals we encounter rarely have any significant effect on the course of our lives. We recognize plenty of faces. We memorize plenty of names. We learn a few small personal details and do our best to keep them all neatly correlated. Yet most of us are destined to remain little more than imperfect strangers to nearly everyone around us. But, every now and then, one of these strangers comes along and, through some marvel of human interaction, becomes *un*strange to us in ways unforeseeably profound. Sometimes we spy this stranger approaching from a distance. Sometimes they appear suddenly, standing right in front of us.

Whatever else might come of them, much literature is born of these transformative encounters. The chance meeting, the crossing of paths, the neat or nasty wake of entanglement: these things are the fuel of fables and folktales, the flaming heart of romance, the source of chills in good ghost stories.

Whatever and whoever these encounters involve, however their details unfold, the most powerful have a way of provoking a confrontation with our own fears and desires, strengths and limitations.

If we're lucky, life marks us with a few good stories of this sort. Some beautiful, some terrifying, and some that leave us forever aching with amazement. Years on, the best remain affirmations that we have not always been so alone or unknown. We are blessed who can say that *this* or *that* stranger once approached—how like a miracle they found us in time—that there was extraordinary power and vitality in the convergence—that something deep within us was awakened or put to rest.

But knowledge so intensely personal can never mean to others what it has meant to us. And there is real danger in attempting to share it.

I have spent years waiting for the right words to come. And still they refuse me. Maybe I should have waited longer. Maybe I waited too long. Or maybe most of what I have to say simply can't be said. In any case, the heart of the matter is this: what animates this little book is the spark of encounter, the shadow of confrontation. Long gone from the senses, the two keep flickering in the mind. Bright moments return. Memory stretches until it snaps in the dark.

How much have I invented? Everything. Nothing. A book of poems. *A book of poems!*

VI

We made a lovely home. We kept a lovely cat. We planted a lovely garden. We had lovely neighbors. We worked and traveled and came home again. We sent and received postcards from around the country, around the world. We decorated a fridge with them. Time passed.

We had a good thing going. We hosted friends and family for meals. We had impromptu get-togethers. We knew what we were about and we enjoyed ourselves. Our place was filled with life and love. And we had plenty of time.

In our living room a miniature painting of an elephant hung on the wall, a hidden message tucked inside. In the crawlspace beneath our bedroom floor a scrabbling family of raccoons came and went. In a hanging plant outside our front door a hummingbird built its nest and left its tiny perfect egg. I wrote a few things I was proud of. Through it all she danced and did her own impressive things. And time passed.

In the end my confidence and optimism unraveled, and with it went my sense of purpose and direction. For whatever reason, the path that seemed possible in the beginning turned out not to be.

In the end our lovely home didn't last. It's the rare home that does.

The week I moved out I got another ticket but this one had nothing to do with street sweeping.

I'd come home from work to find a city crew pouring cement over potholes in the alley behind our apartment. This gave me an idea. I fixed a sandwich in the kitchen, and went back outside to wait for the men to finish. When they drove away, I moved aside their orange cones and caution tape, and began carving into the dark square of cement.

The words I carved had come to me three years before while driving home on the final day of my first classroom teaching job. The job had only been a summer gig, but it was a success and, coasting along through weekend traffic on the 405, I felt incredibly special to be returning to the woman I loved. The sky was thick with clouds and the prospect of summer rain. I rolled my windows down and turned off the stereo to let in the odor of automobile exhaust and the tack of tires turning. I put my hand out to feel the first drops. And the words came like magic. I chanted them to myself the whole way home. When I got back I sat down and laid them out on paper, pleased not to have lost them.

But the mood of this earlier, happier day felt impossibly remote from the afternoon where I now stooped to cut those words into the alley. I was desperate to leave something behind. In a few days I'd be gone from the apartment I shared with the woman I loved. We'd spent five years together. Nearly the whole of that time, up till even the final few months, was characterized by an elegance I knew she infused into it.

Was I certain I wanted to leave? She'd put this question to me a week earlier. It was a generous gift, a peace offering, a real chance to reconsider. Somehow it made me even more desperate. I loved her of course. But I'd set a ball rolling. That I may have been capable of stopping it or altering its course wouldn't occur to me until much later.

Meanwhile, as I carved a poem into the wet cement, a cop drove up and asked what I was doing. I told him: I was carving a poem into wet cement. He informed me that carving wet cement was illegal, that I was defacing public property.

I didn't know where to begin my defense. I had made each letter as neatly as I could. *What was I defacing?* I asked and gestured to the alley. It was strewn with litter and lined with graffitied garage doors and dirty dumpsters. Besides, wasn't carving into fresh cement outside one's home an American tradition? *Where was the harm?*

He got out of his car for a closer look. I took a deep breath to keep calm. I didn't need more trouble. He explained he was responding to a call from someone in the neighborhood, and that he was bound by law to issue a citation if I continued. I told him I was halfway through and preferred to finish.

I could see he was a kind man, and this made me want to cry out for pity. Might he be willing, as a courtesy, a small act of mercy, to settle with clubbing me a few times and just call it a day? How could I explain what drove me to make these silly marks?

Like a fool, I thanked him for the ticket.

Why was I walking out? *Why* would anyone choose to leave so many good things behind? The question plagued me. So much had been good between us. So much had felt right. But this hardly mattered.

Maybe it had something to do with turning thirty? Maybe it had something to do with settling down, a fear of routine? Maybe it was the discomfort of domesticity, an impatience for vague adventure? Friends were leaving town, getting married, moving away. Talk of marriage and starting a family made me nervous. They felt like delicate operations I might not survive. I just wasn't ready yet. Something about settling made me want to unsettle myself.

What had gotten into me? Some sort of crookedness. A darkness perhaps. I was fighting my own shadow, struggling against a sickening sense of impending failure. The feeling was vague but it loomed in me and gnawed at my heart. She loved me, but even more important she *believed* in me. About these two things I had no doubt. Yet somewhere along the line I lost her same faith in myself.

An idea grew like cancer in my mind: I was going to fail us both. Like a wounded animal, I felt an urge to crawl off some place and disappear.

The thought that I wasn't worthy, the thought of letting her down, of hurting her, of disappointing our friends and family, all of whom recognized there was something special about *us*, the thought of throwing away all the good things we had going together filled me with dread and shame. And still, rather than trying to work through this terrible knot I convinced myself that my leaving would liberate her. It was the oddest and emptiest of consolations.

Like a fool I boxed it up and carried it with me out the door.

VII

In the end, my new place wasn't far from my old place. I was starting over again. For two months, I slept on a thin bedroll on the floor. I did what I could with what I had. When a friend mentioned he was selling his futon bed, I was grateful for the upgrade.

I found a nice old desk on Craigslist. It was wooden, worn and brown. It felt sturdy, and its drawers smelled like inspiration. The desktop lifted to reveal a hideaway typewriter mount I liked but had no use for, and there were two recessed shelves on either side that pulled out like cutting boards and were just large enough to rest a leg or a drink on. I bought an old wooden chair to go with it. It too was simple and brown and fit neatly under the desk, which I positioned in front of a window that looked out on another filthy alley. I didn't mind the view.

I sat at this desk sometimes, writing or rewriting, but nothing on the page was ever as nice as the sunlight that came through my window. For a couple hours each day it brightened the smooth planking of my hardwood floor. Out that window, night or day, there was always something going on in the alley.

One Saturday afternoon in summer, I sat at the desk, studying the brick wall across the way. After a while, voices came bouncing off it. The voices grew louder, talking and joking until their bodies appeared and stopped outside my open window. Then the girl turned and lifted her shirt and bra for the two guys egging her on. Then gasps and laugher as the three walked out of view. Another day I watched a guy in a single fluid graceful movement scale the low wall of the building across the way and vault through an open apartment window and disappear. Once a photographer and a model drove up to use the wall as the backdrop for their fashion shoot. The photographer's car was full of serious equipment. His model had a blue-and-white-striped tube top, golden high-waisted shorts, and thighs like caramel. After a couple wardrobe changes and many poses they packed up and moved on too. Who were these people? Where were they going?

My apartment was old and small, but the building was handsome and in good shape. I propped a couple potted plants against the iron security bars outside my windows. I got to know my neighbors. To my left lived an older man who towed around an oxygen tank. He had a terrible, wracking cough that clattered through the walls and kept us both from sleep. But he was friendly, and lived alone like me, and we greeted each other when we passed in the hallway. I never saw him leave the building further than the front stoop. Occasionally I'd join him there for conversation when I got home from work. Passersby, many of whom my neighbor knew by name, often stopped to talk. And when he learned I was a teacher, he smiled. He'd been a professor once. The job had wrecked his lungs. He told me this as if it made perfect sense. I lived next to him for a year before he said any more about the matter.

One evening on the stoop, he brought it up again. In the mid-eighties, he said, after finishing his doctorate, he'd taught math at UCLA. For a time, he did well for himself. He liked his subject and his students. The hours and pay were good. He began to treat himself to a bit of the finer stuff of life—sharp clothes, good meals out, a nice apartment and new car, live music at fancy nightclubs with pretty women. One night a special lady he was seeing pulled a baggie of cocaine from her purse. Hers was a totally new sort of invitation to consider. He wasn't much of a drinker, just socially, and had never smoked, not even once, not even a cigarette. But god, he adored this woman. So he accepted the pipe when it was passed. She didn't call it crack, though that was the name he came to know it by. That night, the professor told me, was incomprehensibly fantastic. Those hours he spent, most of them in bed with her, were easily the finest, most sensual hours of his entire life. He felt that inside him a lamp he never knew existed had been lit, and suddenly his world became so bright it was as if all his earlier days had been lived in darkness. His big mistake was that he tried to use this lamp to blaze a new way forward. The lamp was too hot and the material of his life caught fire—first the teaching position, then the money, then the apartment, then the woman, and finally his lungs. Everything burned. I was surprised by how little sentimentality there was in his telling of the story. He didn't apologize overmuch. *I made some choices and things happened*, he shrugged. For a time he enjoyed the hell out of himself. He only wished he'd had stronger lungs.

To my right lived another guy, who, by pure coincidence, had grown up around the corner from me in Downey. He was several years older than me and, though we had never been friends, we recognized each other immediately. I even knew his name. Ten years earlier a mutual friend of ours invited me to rent a room in a house in Fullerton after he had asked this guy to move out. The circumstances of that situation had been a bit touchy at the time, but the bizarre improbability of our current situation made us laugh. We were neighbors once again. His studio was the same size shoebox as mine. He lived there with his wife and young daughter and a chihuahua. Within a few months of my moving in, his wife gave birth to their second child.

One day I came home from work and learned the

old professor had died. I was chopping red onion in the kitchen when there was a knock at my door. My neighbor delivered the news with tears in his eyes. His wife, who was fond of the old man and liked to bring the kids over to visit with him, had found him that same morning slumped naked on his bathroom floor. The paramedics figured he must have passed sometime in the middle of the previous night.

Over dinner I thought about the old professor.

I was busy again with work, in the middle of student teaching. Gradually my darkness had been lifting. I found myself becoming distracted again by music, by books, by friends, by bills, by hiking, by cleaning and cooking. And, briefly, by girls.

But that night I determined never to die on a toilet seat in a studio apartment alone.

My citation for defacing public property carried a penalty of several hundred dollars and would get worse if I didn't pay soon. That's what the notices that came in the mail said. I kept these notices piled neatly on a corner of my desk until all my requests for extensions had been exhausted.

At the courthouse I stood in line for an hour. When it was my turn, I passed my ticket under the plexiglass window to the clerk on the other side. She entered the citation's number into her computer, then my first and last name, then slid my ticket back to me. I couldn't hear what she said so I bent my ear closer to the slot where the ticket was. *There is no record for this ticket, sir.* How could that be if I have the ticket here? *Who knows,* she said, *it may have been dismissed by the issuing officer.* But what did that mean now? Her words came clearly through the slot: *No record, no ticket, no fine.*

I thanked her and walked out. On the street I turned left and headed for the beach, where I sat on the sand and meditated on the mystery of grace. This was the best thing to happen to me in a while.

VIII

Nowhere I lived in Long Beach was ever farther than a few blocks from the ocean.

Regardless of the season, the city's main beach always had a desolate feel that I loved. In the winter, I would take my book and a coffee to sit and read in the cool morning sand. In the summer, when the marine layer burned off, I'd ride down on my bike and lay out a towel and nap in the sun. The nearest person might be more than a hundred yards away, their music and conversation warbling unintelligibly over long stretches of sand. Almost nobody swam, but once in a while, just off shore, a fisherman in a sunhat would float by in an innertube. Further out, weekend regattas shifted on the water in sleepy clusters off the pier. Cigarette boats rumbled back and forth past the oil islands. Helicopters and small planes trailing banners or on their way to Catalina buzzed overhead. Under all these sounds was the constant metronomic gasp of breakwater waves tossing themselves onto the sand. There was something maddeningly heroic in the relentlessness of such puny things.

I kept an eye out for needles, fishhooks, and broken bottles when I walked the beach barefoot. One evening I came across a seal near the pier. This was the only seal I ever saw in Long Beach. I got excited. It lay in a sandy depression surrounded by orange mesh. A sign nearby said to leave it alone—it was sick and needed space. It rolled its wet black eyes at me as I passed on my way to meet a few friends for a sundown pint.

When the weather was good, I liked to swim the channel between the Peninsula and Naples. I swam with friends through the canals, climbed up random docks to jump from the walls and bridges. Out in the harbor, we dove from the bow of a sailboat anchored off the oil islands.

I spent a lot of time in the parks just above the beach where I liked to exercise and run the stairs. There was no better place to lay in the grass and chat with strangers or meet up with friends for a picnic. Below the bluff, people I never saw were always raking block-letter messages in the sand: JESUS IS LOVE—HAVE YOU CALLED YOUR MOM TODAY?—ALL WILL BE OKAY—MARRY ME MARY?—DON'T JUMP. Their messages were large and cheerful. Who were these thoughtful people? Were they sincere?

One day a bad fire broke out in the tall blue apartment tower that stands alone on the bluff. A week after the sirens and commotion, I sat reading on the beach. A dozen stories up was the blackened, boarded-up window through which a man had jumped to his death. I considered his dilemma—leap for a chance to live or burn for sure in blistering flames. Such grim choices sent shivers through me. Who was this brave man? Did anyone grieve him?

–

When the gloom sunk back in, as I knew it would, there wasn't much I could do about it. I held my breath. It whelmed in the evenings while I washed dishes in the sink. I was on my own.

But there were also moments when I was visited by intense sensations of beauty. I don't know what else to call them. They came without warning. Sometimes they lasted a few minutes, sometimes an entire morning. Sometimes the better part of an afternoon was supercharged by them. They kept no schedule. They came whenever—while driving to work or back home or riding around town. They came while responding to student writing or exercising at the park, while reading at the coffee shop or out for a walk at sunset. They visited me while I sat side by side students learning their letters, or while I sat in a noisy barroom full of strangers. They reached me like the embrace of a lover. And occasionally they were accompanied by words and phrases, some of which appear in the pages of this book.

IX

The last time I saw her was at an outdoor concert downtown. It was the end of a hot summer and the streets had been given over to music. After debating with myself all evening whether to walk over or not, I arrived in time to catch the closing band. She saw me in the crowd during the lull and came to say hello. We chatted. *How was I doing, how had I been? Had I come by myself?* Her questions were difficult to answer. I smiled and spoke through clenched teeth. More than anything, I wanted to drop to my knees, to soak her pretty shoes with tears, to beg forgiveness. But already she was moving back through the crowd, returning to the people she'd come with.

I was a fool. I should never have come. And now I was trapped in a throng. The band I came to see was muffled by my mind. When the crowd loosened after their last song, I slunk away seething through teeming happy couples. I prayed for a miracle—a flying bullet, a bomb—anything that might kill me quick or leave me trampled by the mob. Was there no maniac in their midst who might plunge a knife into my heart? The streets were clotted with laughter. I watched for passing cars to throw myself in front of but no one was coming to my rescue.

It was too hot to go home. In a daze of despair, I walked until I was looking out over the water. Of what use were these bluffs if I couldn't bring myself to jump?

Eventually, everywhere I turned was mired in memory. The sight of certain streets and buildings and locations I once loved now struck me as unbearably lonesome. More and more, my friends were marrying off, starting families, moving away. I was losing touch with people I loved. I was growing afraid.

Long Beach was becoming a burning building. If I wanted to save myself I would have to jump. But where would I land?

The question brought me back to a conversation I'd had with a professor several years before. It was after finals, during that empty week before graduation, and I had dropped by campus to return a few books. I crossed his path as I exited the library and stopped to thank him again for his class.

I must have been beaming. I was elated to have succeeded in juggling the demands of work and school and a budding relationship, and I'd thrown every damned ounce of myself into those efforts. To top it off, I'd written my longest, most ambitious, and most fulfilling term paper ever for this professor's class. It was the single best piece of writing I'd done up to that point. I was not exaggerating when I told him his class had changed my life. He accepted my compliment graciously, and thanked me for my paper. It was, he said, among the best undergrad work he'd seen, and he was pleased I made good on the extension he'd granted me. I didn't bother mentioning I was twenty-six. We stood chatting a moment before he wondered what my next step was. *What were my plans for after summer?*

I had a few ideas but none were "career-oriented." First, I was going to move in with the girl I was in love with. Then I would continue writing, looking for opportunities to publish, while my girlfriend and I saved money to travel, maybe for a trip around the world, maybe for an extended stay in Mexico or South America to work on our Spanish. He smiled, said he'd done something similar when he was my age, and that he wished me the best of luck. But it was what he said next that stuck. He asked if I had given any thought to grad school? I hadn't. He suggested it might be a good idea after taking some time to pursue the other goals. He said I showed promise.

Until this comment, I had never given a single serious thought to a master's program. Hell, not long before, I was still worried I might not make it through college at all. I was relieved just to be graduating. But his suggestion took root in my mind. For six years it germinated. Whenever I felt down on myself, I would think back on this conversation, his comment—*I showed promise*—and take comfort in at least one person's belief that I might be good enough to carry my studies forward.

It was the memory of this comment that helped set my mind right following the implosion of a final, brief relationship. I realized it was time to leave Long Beach. There was no future for me here anymore. The building was on fire. But I'd survived fires before.

I started researching graduate programs and putting in applications to schools in places I thought I might like to live. I trusted at least one would accept me. And since I was leaving, I figured I might as well do it right. There was no reason to wait around for acceptances. I would wander awhile, work on my Spanish, take time for myself. I had saved money, and work could be found wherever I landed.

After submitting my last application, I bought a one-way flight out of the country. I could figure out my return flight later.

~

Three months before I left, I went for a bike ride down to the Peninsula with a girl I thought I knew. We sat in the sand, passing a bottle of beer back and forth, debating whether to swim or not. It was getting late, but we'd brought our suits. It would be a shame to leave without getting wet.

So we changed and waded in. The water was dark and chill. I stuffed my wallet in my shoes and removed my ring and zipped it in my shorts. Looking up at the sun going down we counted to three and dove under together. We swam across to Naples, climbed a dock, jumped from the wall, and swam back. Though we swam side by side the whole way, the two of us couldn't have been further apart.

On our ride back along the beach path, I trailed behind and watched her silhouette against the fading light of the harbor. I pedaled in silence, fixed on the beauty of a place I had known and loved.

Near the end of my time in Long Beach, with the help of friends, I organized a holiday party. We hung my apartment walls with the work of a painter friend, and my living room floor became a stage for musicians. To my great delight, people came from out of town, out of state, even out of the country. Old friends and new, older students and younger ones with their families filled my apartment. The company lasted till very late. Throughout the night I felt happier than I'd felt in months, maybe years. I wasn't alone. We had so much fun we threw a second party two weeks later.

That night I started giving things away. I put books into the hands of individuals who I figured might enjoy them. I put potted plants into hands that might keep them alive. If someone asked about something on a shelf, I invited them to take it when they left.

To get rid of the rest of my stuff I had a yard sale. I

made a little money but not much. After most of the big stuff sold, I started sending items off with whoever expressed interest in them. The very last thing I sold was my little car. I wouldn't need it where I was going.

~

While tying up the last few loose ends, I realized my grandfather's ring was missing. But I didn't freak out. I had gone through this before. It would turn up in the final cleaning of my apartment, I knew. But I searched for it everywhere and it didn't turn up. Could it have fallen down the open drain in my bathroom sink? I'd gotten into a bad habit of setting it in the soap dish on the sink's edge. Why was I always being so damn lazy and foolish? I peered down the sink's stopper-less black hole with a flashlight. Nothing. I'd been so distracted the last couple months I couldn't remember the last time I'd worn it. Could it have been stolen during one of the parties? But who would have stolen it?

The closer I got to leaving, the more desperate I got to find that ring. In my final days I scoured my apartment. I triple and quadruple-checked anywhere it might be. It wasn't in a corner of my closet. It hadn't fallen into any kitchen drawers and it wasn't sitting on any cupboard shelves. Could it have slipped between the cushions of the couch I sold? Did I now have to count the loss of my ring among all the other losses crowding my mind? What sort of shitty omen was this?

In the end, I gave up. The best thing to do was move on.

I left my apartment as empty and unrecognizably mine as the day I first walked into it.

X

At some point during all this, I promised myself I would make a monument to this period in my life, to preserve something about the people and experiences that formed me during it. Longing compelled me to finish the task—longing to go back in time, to live certain moments again: a few hours of morning here, a stretch of afternoon there, complete days and whole weeks somewhere else. I wanted to make immortal everyone and everything I have ever loved, and to keep them near in ways I never could do when they were close. I wanted to say thanks, to seek forgiveness, to say a better goodbye. I wish I knew whether such longing is common. I know only of my own.

Out of respect, I have kept names out of this. But hardly a day has passed that I haven't thought of her. Once in a while she still appears in my dreams. These dreams are among the happiest and most agonizing I have known. Of course, I know enough about dreams to know it is not *she* who visits me, but rather something deep within me that takes her shape and face and voice. Nevertheless, in these dreams I am waking and she is there. It is early morning and she stirs beside me, soft and warm under the covers. Or it is evening. And, like a hero in an old movie, I am walking triumphantly back into the life we once shared. In each scene, I find her lovelier than when I left her. In these dreams we have not aged. We are what we were.

At times the ache of these dreams is so fantastically exquisite it shakes me from sleep. Rolling over in bed, I have to open my eyes to snuff the longing in my heart. Alone in the dark, I imagine something awful within me—cowardice or courage—keeps me tending these secret fires. These dreams come less often these days, and for this I am grateful. I tell myself they are just another reminder that I live, that I have known uncommon love.

I got on the plane. I traveled through months, walked strange streets, met new people, filled myself with new experiences. Little by little life settled back into place. Less and less I mistook the angles of her face in the profiles of passengers on trains. Less and less my heart snared in chance resemblances—an identical head of hair and height, a certain sway in someone's step alongside me on the sidewalk, the sound of her name in the mouths of passersby. Time passed. I began to feel better.

Early one morning I got out of bed in the dark, dressed and headed out to a small park I passed by the day before. I felt like exercising and the park sat at the top of a hill I thought might provide a decent view. The town was small and I made my way by memory back through its streets and up a flight of stairs. The park wasn't much to look at—a warped metal slide, some monkey bars, a swing set, a few bent benches planted in the dirt around patchy grass. But the view—a grid of terra cotta roofs dark with dew and moss. In the distance, clouds on green hills and mist in the valleys.

I took my time and stretched. I did push-ups, sit-ups, and pull-ups. I nodded hello to occasional passersby and their dogs. Everything that morning was pleasant and agreeable. I hadn't exercised since leaving Long Beach.

As I went through my simple circuit, I wandered back over the path that had led me here—to the park on this hilltop, to this small town in this strange country. The last few months seemed an improbable span of time for so much change. I knew most of that change— the change of scenery, the adjustment of language and culture, the shift in routine, the loosening of worry and self-doubt—was only temporary. But what wasn't? Besides, even the most fleeting experience could leave long-lasting impressions. I watched the clouds sweep slowly over the hills. What new impressions would the next months bring?

Eventually my thoughts turned to breakfast. Had I grabbed enough cash before leaving my room? I pulled a folded bill and some coins from my shorts pocket. Wedged deep down, the smaller coins clinked as I fished them out. And there in my open hand, mixed with dull pesos, was my gold ring.

For a moment I froze and stared in disbelief. I laughed out loud. I was a damned fool! I wanted to slap myself. Instead I slipped the ring back on. And, with something like a prayer in mind, I floated down the long flight of stairs to breakfast.

So it goes. The story continues as complicated as it is unexceptional. It is full of holes and gaps. It's missing many facts and faces I don't have the heart or talent to portray faithfully here. Perhaps somewhere down the line I may return to them. Maybe I will. Probably I won't.

All told, not much has changed, except everything. I realize in some ways I haven't gone very far at all. But there are days when I am reminded I've come a hell of a long way.

Perhaps it's fitting that I'm typing all this up against a wall in another studio apartment. As I finish, out my window the world has entered a new age of plague and handwringing. Inside I am finally laying down my scourge.

Not long ago I was in Long Beach again with old friends. Most of us live in other cities now but we all came back to watch a performance by the couple musicians among us. They played old songs and new. Each sounded great.

Afterward we crowded into a couple tables at a bar up the street and carried on laughing and catching up over pitchers of beer. We were in high spirits, somewhere near exultant. And when our group thinned as it got later the rest of us squeezed into a booth to close the place down. At last we shuffled out and stood on the corner wrapping up stories and finishing conversations before we said goodnight.

It was a long walk downtown to the hotel room I was staying in, but fortunately I had a friend to walk with. Side by side we walked and wondered about many things. He had lived here too and understood. It was late and quiet so we talked softly as we passed old places we knew. Here and there we noted changes to the neighborhood, old businesses replaced, new buildings going up.

Turning a corner, I saw a light in a window I used to look out of. How many nights and days had that light shined for me? All of a sudden that bright room, all the dark streets outside—*everything*—trembled in me like scenes from a book I loved but would never read again. I felt unspeakably old and strange, and something inside me shook like sobbing or waves, shivering or song.

At 2nd Street and Alamitos we turned down an alley I had cut through many times. It was a short, narrow stretch with a tucked-away quality I'd always liked. Halfway in it hid a modest cottage, kept like a secret from decades of development. Within the year both the alley and its cottage would be cleared away to make room for another crisp stack of condos. Today they exist only in memories and old maps.

But that alley that night looked exactly as I remembered it. And we made our way through it over potholes and crumbling concrete. If not for the light of a triggered flood lamp I might have tripped on a piece of chalk. It had been left behind by kids whose drawings covered the cement. Their work was from earlier that day, and we stopped a moment to take it in. It was a sprawling panorama in the spirit of summer—with a smiling sun and curlicue clouds, colorful birds and bright flowers, and a few stick figures dancing near the ocean's edge. The scene was so refreshingly naïve it made me want to cheer. This was a thing of exuberance and beauty in an otherwise forgotten passage. So what if its color wouldn't last?

We continued on a few steps before I stopped and turned back for the chalk I'd kicked. It was the extra thick kind and I tossed it in my hand a couple times to test its powdery blue weight. It was impossibly light. So I used it to write a message on the ground: WE WERE HERE

Then we moved on.

I wonder if you live there still
I kinda think you always will
If I tried, you'd probably be hard to find

The National
"Hard to Find"

~

3rd & Orange

Thank you

CPSIA information can be obtained
at www.ICGtesting.com
Printed in the USA
LVHW100300230522
719465LV00015B/211